Morning Break

and other poems

Wes Magee

Illustrations by Valeria Petrone

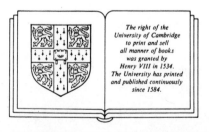

The right of the
University of Cambridge
to print and sell
all manner of books
was granted by
Henry VIII in 1534.
The University has printed
and published continuously
since 1584.

CAMBRIDGE UNIVERSITY PRESS

Cambridge
New York   New Rochelle
Melbourne   Sydney

For Liz,

Enjoy these poems!

Wes Magee

£1991

for Kingsley

Published by the Press Syndicate of the University of Cambridge
The Pitt Building, Trumpington Street, Cambridge CB2 1RP
32 East 57th Street, New York, NY 10022, USA
10 Stamford Road, Oakleigh, Melbourne 3166, Australia

© Cambridge University Press 1989

First published 1989

Printed in Great Britain at the University Press, Cambridge

British Library cataloguing in publication data

Magee, Wes
   Morning break and other poems.
   I. Title
   821'.914

Library of Congress cataloging-in-publication data

Magee, Wes 1939 –
   Morning Break, and other poems/Wes Magee.
   1. Children's poetry, English. [1. English poetry.]   I. Title.
   PR6063. A328M67 1988
   821'.914–dc19   88–14984

ISBN 0 521 36118 4 hard covers
ISBN 0 521 36940 1 paperback

GO

Contents

Morning break

Andrew Flag plays football
Jane swings from the bars
Chucker Peach climbs drainpipes
Spike is seeing stars

Little Paul's a Martian
Anne walks on her toes
Ian Dump fights Kenny
Russell picks his nose

Dopey Di does hopscotch
Curly drives a train
Maddox-Brown and Lai Ching
Stuff shoes down the drain

Lisa Thin throws netballs
Ranji stands and stares
Nuttall from the first year
Shouts and spits and swears

Dick Fish fires his ray gun
Gaz has stamps to swop
Dave and Dan are robbers
Teacher is the cop

Betty Blob pulls faces
Basher falls . . . and dies
Tracey shows her knickers
Loony swallows flies

Faye sits in a puddle
Trev is eating mud
Skinhead has a nose bleed –
pints and pints of blood

Robbo Lump pings marbles
Ahmed hands out cake
What a lot of nonsense
During
         Morning
                  Break

An accident

The playground noise stilled.
A teacher ran to the spot
beneath the climbing frame
where Rawinda lay, motionless.
We crowded around, silent,
gazing at the trickle of blood
oozing its way onto the tarmac.
Red-faced, the teacher shouted,
'Move back . . . get out of the way!'
and carried Rawinda into school,
limbs floppy as a rag doll's,
a red gash on her black face.

Later we heard she was at home,
five stitches in her forehead.
After school that day
Jane and I stopped beside the frame
and stared at the dark stain
shaped like a map of Ireland.
'Doesn't look much like blood,'
muttered Jane. I shrugged,
and remember now how warm it was
that afternoon, the white clouds,
and how sunlight glinted
from the polished bars.

We took Rawinda's 'Get Well' card
to her house. She was in bed,
quiet, propped up on pillows,
a white plaster on her dark skin.
Three days later
she was back at school,
her usual self, laughing,
twirling expertly on the bars,
wearing her plaster with pride,
covering for a week the scar
she would keep for ever,
memento of a July day at school.

teacher teacher

teacher teacher
you're the best
when you wear
that old string vest

teacher teacher
come here quick
Stella Brown's
been awful sick

teacher teacher
no more school
let's go down
the swimming pool

teacher teacher
I'm off home
got to feed my
garden gnome

The silent teacher

My teacher, Mr Raven-Black,
he never says a word
yet he makes sure, oh yes indeed,
his orders are all *heard*.

In class you'll never hear him speak;
he talks . . . with *just his hand*,
makes finger signs and signals
that we all understand.

His index finger, beckoning,
means, 'Come and see me . . . now!'
While hands clapped around his ears
is, 'Stop that awful row!'

That finger wagging to and fro
says, 'Stop it, silly twit!'
And both hands pressing slowly down
just order us to . . . sit.

One hand slapped upon his brow
tells you . . . he's had enough.
That straight-out, pointing finger
demands, 'Who left . . . this *stuff*?'

One finger placed across his lips
says, 'Quiet . . . quiet . . . hush.'
(And once I watched his careful hands
cradle a wounded thrush.)

He often uses fingers crossed
to let us know . . . here's hoping.
But one hand covering his eyes
tells us . . . that he's not coping.

He raises hands above his head
   . . . surrenders . . . once each week.
And one hand cupped behind his ear
is, 'Did I hear . . . some cheek?'

His favourite sign is both thumbs up
to tell us we're okay.
His hand extended near the door
says . . . that's all for today.

My teacher, Mr Raven-Black,
is great with signals, signs.
You'll never hear him moan or groan,
he never shouts or whines.

He's the best teacher in the school.
He'll never get the sack.
Let's put two hands together for
   Mr Raven-Black.

Hymns, not hers

Every morning we file into Hall
forbidden to giggle, talk or call.
Posters from France are stuck on the wall.
Assembly . . . the same old pattern recurs
     and we sing Hymns,
        not *hers*.

'Good morning, pupils,' but the mike won't work
until my teacher gives the cable a jerk.
The electric clock is going berserk
as, like a cat, it spits and purrs
     and we sing Hymns,
        not *hers*.

The daily orders . . . keep quiet, sit still,
you can't, you won't, you *must* not, you will!
Joan whispers to me, 'I'm feeling ill,'
and she's turned the colour of chartreuse
     and we sing Hymns,
        not *hers*.

'Hicks, sit *down* upon your sit-upon!'
Our old Headteacher drones on and on.
Her grey permed hair has almost gone.
Miss at the piano. On chairs, the Sirs
     and we sing Hymns,
        not *hers*.

Next, we're told to keep off the field.
Then, the football team has won a shield.
'They performed well, they did not yield.
Played like professionals, not *amateurs*!'
     And we sing Hymns,
        not *hers*.

The Head cracks a joke. Jeff Biggins howls.
Mrs Glum looks cross and shakes her jowls.
Outside it's raining. Thunder growls.
My view from the Hall window blurs
        and we sing Hymns,
            not *hers*.

It ends, and we exit line by line.
First years, second years, boys . . . then mine.
One more, just *one more hymn* . . . and I'll resign!
But, girls, perhaps it's not so grim,
        one day we'll sing a Her
            for Him!

On Monday morning

There's been a break-in
    down at the school
and our classroom's been wrecked
    by some stupid fool.

The police have arrived
    all smart-dressed and slim.
Our teachers are cross.
    The Head's looking grim.

Six windows are broken.
    We must wait in the Hall.
But there's nothing to do
    so we stare at the wall.

They've paint-sprayed the desks,
    thrown books on the floor,
snapped off all our plants
    and kicked in the door.

That room was our home,
    we worked there with pride
but now it's a wreck
    and we can't go inside.

Detectives are searching
    for footprints and clues.
We're still in our coats
    and full of the blues.

One girl's heard a rumour,
    she gives name and address.
Now the caretaker's here
    to clear up the mess.

Much later that morning
    we're back in our place.
Card over the windows.
    It's all a disgrace.

The vandals stole pens.
    Our hamster's not fed.
There's pain in my heart,
    an ache in my head.

There's been a break-in
    down at the school
and our classroom's been wrecked
    by some stupid fool.

Headteachers . . . at Assembly

This one
jangles a bunch of keys in his pocket,
hates bad behaviour, talks about 'serious cases'.
He stands very close to the front row and once,
during prayers, a boy untied his shoe laces.
The Head turned, tripped, fell to the floor.
There were smiles on all our faces.

This one
is a Great Lady. She wears a knitted shawl
and is always at the hairdresser's: hates muck.
When she holds up items of Lost Property
she shudders in horror and says, 'Yeeeerh! Yuk!'
Socks, shorts or underpants are *never* claimed.
She makes noises like a hen . . . cluck, cluck, cluck.

This one
wears snazzy ties and toeless sandals.
He has nicknames for everyone . . . like Grub, Wombat, or Mad.
If you drop your recorder he'll say,
'You know, that's a hanging offence, lad!'
He winks, does funny walks, and his jokes
are the world's worst . . . really, really bad.

This one
paces up and down like a caged tigress,
her face red as an overripe tomato.
She goes crazy if she hears a cough
and shouts, 'No coughing! *No coughing!* NO!'
But someone coughs, then another: an avalanche of coughs.
Her nose turns crimson and starts to glow.

This one
we call Hitler. He rants and raves every day
and his hair is slicked down flat on his head.
His suits are black, his shoes glassy black,
but his eyes have a suspicious tinge of red.
He fancies our Miss Squash; tells us to rise early,
clean our teeth, and make the bed.

This one
is everyone's friend, knows all our names
and never forgets a birthday.
She whispers so softly that no one can hear a word!
Her hair and eyebrows are totally grey.
When I lost a pound coin she replaced it!
I'll remember that to my dying day.

Who?

'Who,' asked my mother,
'helped themselves to the *new* loaf?'
   My two friends and I
   looked at her
   and shrugged.

'Who,' questioned my mother,
'broke off the crust?'
   Three pairs of eyes
   stared at the loaf
   lying on the kitchen table.

'Who,' demanded my mother,
'ate the bread?'
   No one replied.
   You could hear
   the kitchen clock. Tick. Tock.

And
even now I can taste it,
crisp, fresh, warm from the bakery,
   and I'd eat it again
   if I could find a loaf
   like that, like that . . .

Questions . . . and answers

(a boy's version)

Where's the rattle I shook
when I was 1?
   Vanished.

Where's the Teddy I hugged
when I was 2?
   Lost.

Where's the sand-box I played in
when I was 3?
   Broken up.

Where's the beach ball I kicked
when I was 4?
   Burst.

Where's the fort I built
when I was 5?
   Destroyed.

Where's the box of comics I collected
when I was 6?
   Missing.

Where's the electric train set I loved
when I was 7?
   Given away.

Where's the holiday scrap-book I made
when I was 8?
   Disappeared.

Where's the tin of marbles I had
when I was 9?
   Swopped.

Where's the bicycle I rode
when I was 10?
   Sold.

What, all gone,
everything?
   Yes, all gone,
   all gone . . .

A girl's questions

Mum,
where's my old doll,
the one that cried?
Where's my rocking horse,
and the garden slide?
I don't know.

Dad,
where's my jigsaw,
and my squeaky pram?
Where's old Panda
and my cuddly lamb?
I don't know.

Gran,
where's the dolls' house
Grandad built for me?
Where's the angel
from the Christmas tree?
I don't know.

Sad,
but I've outgrown them,
I suppose.
I've put them aside
like cast-off clothes.

But
the saddest thing
as older you grow
is to hear words like
I don't know.

Gran's green parrot

It was high summer.
Age 9 I travelled alone
to stay at Gran's.
'ello 'ello 'ello 'ello
screeched her green parrot
when I entered the front room
and gazed up at the huge cage
perched high on a wooden pedestal.

That amazing parrot!
Its shrill whistle
pierced your eardrums.
It scattered sunflower seeds
halfway across the carpet
and then climbed around
and around its cage
cackling like a crackpot!

'oo's that? 'oo's that?
it squealed when my father
arrived to take me home.
Just watch this, said dad,
and poked his finger at the cage.
The parrot raced along its perch
and flew at him in a rage.
Dad's finger jabbed closer, closer.

Furious, Gran's green parrot shrieked
at that teasing finger
until, like lightning,
it struck at dad's flesh.
That black beak . . . wearing blood-red lipstick!
Dad tore around and around
Gran's front room
hollering like a hooligan!

Until Gran died

The minnows I caught
lived for a few days in a jar
then floated side-up on the surface.
We buried them beneath the hedge.
I didn't cry, but felt sad inside.

> I thought
> I could deal with funerals,
> that is until Gran died.

The goldfish I kept in a bowl
passed away with old age.
Mum wrapped him in newspaper
and we buried him next to a rose bush.
I didn't cry, but felt sad inside.

> I thought
> I could deal with funerals,
> that is until Gran died.

My cat lay stiff in a shoe box
after being hit by a car.
Dad dug a hole and we buried her
under the apple tree.
I didn't cry, but felt *very* sad inside.

> I thought
> I could deal with funerals,
> that is until Gran died.

And when she died
I went to the funeral
with relations dressed in black.
They cried, and so did I.
Salty tears ran down my face. Oh, how I cried.

> Yes, I thought
> I could deal with funerals,
> that is until Gran died.

She was buried in a graveyard
and even the sky wept that day.
Rain fell and fell and fell,
and thunder sobbed far away across the town.
I cried and I cried.

I thought
I could deal with funerals,
that is until Gran
died.

The man next door

The man next door lives alone
and last year he had a stroke.
He can't talk now, but listens
    when I tell him a joke.

Every day he slowly walks
to the food store down our street.
Every day even if there's
    rain or hail or sleet.

The man next door is silent
and his clothes are in a state.
Mum sends me round on Sundays
    with dinner on a plate.

He sits in his back garden
until the sunlight's gone.
I'm his only visitor.
    Mum says, 'He's got no one'.

The man next door is patient
as the long days come and go.
The world's troubles pass him by:
    a lesson there, you know.

Big Aunt Flo'

Every Sunday afternoon
She visits us for tea
And weighs in somewhere between
A rhino and a flea.
          (But closer to the rhino!)

Aunt Flo' tucks into doughnuts,
Eats fruit cake by the tin.
Her stomach makes strange noises
Just like my rude friend, Flynn.
          (Sounds more like a goat, really!)

Then after tea she heads for
The best chair in the room
And crashes on the cushions
With one resounding boom.
          (You'd think a door had slammed!)

Flo' sits on knitting needles
And snaps them with a crack.
She squashes dolls and jigsaws
Behind her massive back.
          (And she doesn't feel a thing!)

But Aunt Flo' learned a lesson,
There's no doubt about that,
Last Sunday when she grabbed the chair
And sat down on our cat.
          (Big Tom, a cat with a temper!)

The beast let out a wild yell
And dug his claws in . . . deep.
Poor Flo' clutched her huge behind
And gave a massive leap.
          (She almost reached the ceiling!)

So now at Sunday teatime
Jam doughnuts going spare;
Dad winks, and asks where Flo' is
While Tom sleeps on *that* chair.
          (And he's purring, the devil!)

At Aunt Lil's

At Aunt Lil's
there's her lumpy sofa,
a bed-warming pan hanging on the wall,
coloured rugs, a blazing fire,
a hat-stand with antlers in the hall
. . . and
    brown
      sauce
        sandwiches!

At Aunt Lil's
there's my uncle's gold fob watch,
old sepia photos, doorsteps of toast,
her yellow canary, two kittens,
and on the dark stairs . . . a ghost
. . . and
    brown
      sauce
        sandwiches!

At Aunt Lil's
it's old fashioned – no video or TV,
none of 'that rock 'n' roll row!'
It's quiet, very *very* quiet,
but I'll go there *now*
. . . for her world famous
    brown
      sauce
        sandwiches!

Growing up?

It must be
a month or more
since they complained
about the way I eat

or crisps dropped
on the kitchen floor

or not washing my feet

or the TV left blaring
when I go out

or how loudly I shout

or my unmade bed
or mud on the stair

or the soap left to drown
or the state of my hair . . .

It *must* be
a month or more.
Have they given up
in despair?

For years they've
nagged me,
told me to grow up
and act my age.

Has it happened?
Am I now
about to step
onto the stage?

the electronic house

cooker blanket
  toothbrush fire
iron light-bulb
  tv drier
fridge radio
  robot drill
crimper speaker
  kettle grill
slicer grinder
  meters fan
slide-projector
  deep-fry pan
vacuum-cleaner
  fuses shocks
freezer shaver
  junction-box
water-heater
  Christmas lamps
knife recorder
  cables amps
door-chimes organ
  infra-red
guitar video
  sunlamp bed
synthesizer
  night-light glow
cultivator
  stereo
calculator
  metronome
toaster Teasmade
  ohm sweet ohm

Mix-a-Bix

You've never seen
such arms and legs,
there must be thirty-six.
Two eyes on top
and ten behind
confuse the Mix-a-Bix.

Odd Mix-a-Bix from Alpha Six
a case for the Psychiatrix.

With toes on ears
And hairy teeth,
a ghastly, mixed-up freak.
One vest per leg,
house-bricks for food,
and watch out for that beak!

Strange Mix-a-Bix from Alpha Six
a case for the Psychiatrix.

Drinks petrol with
a knife and fork
at least ten times per night.
I've seen its nose
flash on and off
like an electric light.

Mad Mix-a-Bix from Alpha Six
a case for the Psychiatrix.

This space beast is
the worst to sketch;
it's one huge jumbled mess.
And where it sleeps
or how it moves
I can't begin to guess.

Daft Mix-a-Bix from Alpha Six
a case for the Psychiatrix.

the fungus fingers

where the icebergs break in splinters
where the glaciers melt and flow
where the snow is deep as houses
    there the fungus fingers go

where the lightning rips the sky cloth
where the sunburst blinds your eye
where the rain dissolves high mountains
    there the fungus fingers fly

where the islands drown in oceans
where the monsters growl and call
where the forests shake with anger
    there the fungus fingers crawl

where the Space Police are wide-eyed
where the skulls dry in the sun
where the laser beams split planets
    there the fungus fingers run

where the echoes boom through valleys
where the ghostly shadows creep
where the night falls like a hammer
    there
    the
    fungus
    fingers
    LEAP!

The Howler of the Purple Planet

Far beyond our Solar System
Where exists no ray of light
Spins the fog-wrapped Purple Planet
    In an endless night.

Space Police when passing Purple –
on the watch for Killer Zeds –
Heard a fearsome, ice-cold howling
    Deep inside their heads.

Men had never been to Purple,
Never flown down through its fog.
Was the howling caused by gales or
    By a mutant dog?

As the probe-ship hurtled onward
Leaving Purple far behind
So the howling echoed madly
    Through each spaceman's mind.

One man's blood was turned to water,
Three more were quite soon to die,
All because they'd heard that ghostly,
    Disembodied cry.

Far beyond our Solar System
Where exists no ray of light
Spins the fog-wrapped Purple Planet
    In an endless night.

The House on the Hill

It was built years ago
by someone quite manic
and sends those who go there
away in blind panic.
They tell tales of horrors
that can injure or kill
designed by the madman
who lived on the hill.

> If you visit the House on the Hill for a dare
> remember my words . . .
>
> > 'There are dangers. Beware!'

The piano's white teeth
when you plonk out a note
will bite off your fingers
then reach for your throat.
The living-room curtains –
long, heavy and black –
will wrap you in cobwebs
if you're slow to step back.

> If you enter the House on the Hill for a dare
> remember my words . . .
>
> > 'There are dangers. Beware!'

The fridge in the kitchen
has a self-closing door.
If it knocks you inside
then you're ice cubes . . . for sure.
The steps to the cellar
are littered with bones,
and up from the darkness
drift creakings and groans.

> If you go to the House on the Hill for a dare
> remember my words . . .
>
> > 'There are dangers. Beware!'

Turn on the hot tap
and the bathroom will flood
not with gallons of water
but litres of blood.
The rocking-chair's arms
can squeeze you to death;
a waste of time shouting
as you run . . . out . . . of . . . breath.

Don't say you weren't warned or told to take care
when you entered the House on the Hill . . .

for a dare.

The game . . . at the Hallowe'en party in Hangman's Wood

Around the trees ran witches
their nails as long as knives.
Behind a bush hid demons
in fear for their lives.

> Murder, murder in the dark!
> The screams ring in your ears.
> It's just a game, a silly lark,
> no need for floods of tears.

Tall ghosts and other nasties
jumped out and wailed like trains.
A skeleton in irons
kept rattling his chains.

> Murder, murder in the dark!
> The screams ring in your ears.
> It's just a game, a silly lark,
> so wipe away those tears.

A werewolf howled his heart out.
The Horrid Dwarf crept by.
There was blood upon his boots
and murder in his eye.

> Murder, murder in the dark!
> The screams ring in your ears.
> It's just a game, a silly lark,
> Oh, come now, no more tears.

Owls were hooting, 'Is it you?'
Until a wizard grim
pointed to the Dwarf and said,
'The murderer, it's him!'

Murder, murder in the dark!
The screams ring in your ears.
It's just a game, a silly lark,
there's no time left for tears.

Murder, murder in the dark!
The screams fade in the night.
Listen, there's a farm dog's bark!
And look, the dawn's first light!

Sunday morning

Sunday morning
                    and the Sun
                    bawls
                    with his
                    big mouth.

Yachts

                    paper triangles
                    of white and blue
                    crowd
                    the sloping bay
                    as if placed there
                    by an infant hand

                    beneath a shouting sky

                    upon a painted sea.

The signal

It catches your eye
that sudden flash
of sunlight
from the window
in a distant
block of flats.

Again, the signal,
a seasonal message
to say
spring has arrived,
the cold winter
gone.

Now the air warms,
birds yammer
ceaselessly,
leaves and
blades of grass
yawn, stretch.

Perhaps once a year
it catches your eye,
that sudden
flash of sunlight
from a
distant window.

The woodland haiku

Fox

Slinks to the wood's edge
and – with one paw raised – surveys
the open meadows.

Fallow deer

Moves as smooth as smoke
and starts at an air tremor.
Is gone like a ghost.

Rabbits

Blind panic sets in
and they're off; dodgem cars
gone out of control.

Rooks

They float high above,
black as scraps of charred paper
drifting from a fire.

Owl

Blip on his radar
sends owl whooshing through the dark,
homing in on mice, rats.

Pike

Killer submarine
he lurks deep in the woodland's
green-skinned pond. Lurks . . . waits.

Sheep's skull

Whitened and toothless,
discovered in a damp ditch.
A trophy for home.

Humans

Clumsy, twig-snapping,
they see nothing but trees, trees.
The creatures hide . . . watch . . .

A British garden

The SPRING garden is *Irish* green,
its forty shades ranging
from the emerald stems of tulips
to the lawn's striped lemon and lime.
Already the garden is looking spruce,
a daffodil buttonhole on its jacket.
At gloaming see the crocus candles,
tiny flames of azure and crimson.

The SUMMER garden is *Welsh* dragon-red,
roses vivid as blood blots in the borders
while sunflowers beam down on leeks.
We lie beneath leafy trees slowly toasting,
first salmon-pink then lobster.
Red hot pokers stoke up the heat.
At evening look westward,
see how the sky runs with cochineal.

The AUTUMN garden is *Scots* tartan,
a blend of russet, gold and blue.
The trees wear plaid overcoats.
Soon, bonfires at garden ends,
then skirls of smoke, kilts of flame.
The clans gather for roast chestnuts,
watch fireworks shed their silver stars.
The children squeal and screech like bagpipes.

The WINTER garden is *English* white,
a cool bride who prepares herself
for a ceremony of pure cold.
Her snow gown dazzles with frost sequins.
The garden waterfall is iced like a
many-tiered wedding cake. A silence,
before the guests celebrate.
Children hurl white meringues against walls.

The old tree stump

The old stump
is all that remains
of an elm tree
felled years ago.
Now it's our garden seat
comfortably covered
with a moss cushion
upon which our cat
sleeps in the sun.

A dead stump?
Peel back the bark
and see scores of ants
swarming like Londoners
in the rush hour,
or watch the woodlice
trundling like army tanks
to the front line
of some forgotten war.

And here's a centipede
plunging down a crack
like a potholer
exploring unknown caverns.
Later, when we've gone,
a thrush alights
and uses the stump as an anvil
upon which to smash
a land snail's shell.

It's a favourite spot
in our garden,
this old tree stump,
and – you know –
it's quite the best
place to sit
and sun yourself
on a sweltering day
in the middle of July.

Up on the Downs

Up on the Downs,
Up on the Downs,
A skylark flutters
And the fox barks shrill,
Brown rabbit scutters
And the hawk hangs still.
Up on the Downs,
Up on the Downs,
With butterflies
    jigging
        like
            costumed
                clowns.

Here in the Hills,
Here in the Hills,
The long grass flashes
And the sky seems vast,
Rock lizard dashes
And a crow flies past.
Here in the Hills,
Here in the Hills,
With bumble bees
    buzzing
        like
            high-speed
                drills.

High on the Heath,
High on the Heath,
The slow-worm slithers
And the trees are few,
Field-mouse dithers
And the speedwell's blue.
High on the Heath,
High on the Heath,
Where grasshoppers
chirp
in the
grass
beneath.

A blue day

The sky was perfect, an unblemished blue,
and the sun shone like a polished gold coin
     for the day of our picnic.
In a meadow dotted with speedwell and harebells
we spread a tablecloth and unpacked our food.
     A sumptuous feast!

Later we walked through a wood,
a still and shady place where we gazed
     at acres of nodding bluebells.
Then paddled in a stream while minnows
darted nervously. Suddenly, a kingfisher's
     electric, sapphire flash!

Usually a 'blue day' denotes sadness,
but our picnic was a memory to store against
     the dark days of December.
It was a day abuzz with life
when no one cried, and laughter was heard
     under a perfect blue sky.

A hot day at the school

All day long the sun glared
as fiercely as a cross Headteacher.

Out on the brown, parched field
we trained hard for next week's Sports Day.

Hedges wilted in the heat;
teachers' cars sweltered on the tarmac.

In the distance, a grenade of thunder
exploded across the glass sky.

Sprots Day

It's Friday at last,
it's pouring with rain.
The sky is grey and
it's Sports Day again.

My trainers are clean.
I'm in team colour 'Red'.
Our mascot – Old Sam –
has one ear on his head.

All morning it pours.
It just isn't fair.
We're all fed up and
the teachers despair.

By lunchtime it's clear,
sun breaks through the cloud.
Chairs onto the field.
We're expecting a crowd.

The loud-speaker's tested,
first-aid tent goes up.
We carry out ropes,
the Shield and the Cup.

Programmes are ready –
what an error to make!
Someone has printed
'*Sprots* Day' by mistake!

By one-thirty we're out
parading in teams.
We can clap, we can cheer
but no booing or screams.

The grass is still wet.
Parents sit in their rows.
Everything's set. Bang!
The starting gun goes.

First race is sprinting
but way down the track
one of the runners
is flat on his back.

Then it's the sack race.
They all start off . . . fast.
Henry's the leader,
poor Lorna is last.

But, wait, what's all this?
That Lorna's a cheat!
Her sack's got two holes
and she wins . . . on her feet!

The obstacle race
is good for a laugh.
You roll on a mat
and leap-frog the staff.

Team scores are announced.
Not one single cheer.
The speaker's switched off
and no one can hear.

We buy bags of crisps,
swig drinks from a can.
Listen! What's that?
It's Mick's ice-cream van!

Parents judge races;
first, second and third.
They get it all wrong
and protests are heard.

A blackboard shows scores,
tells you who's in the lead.
It falls on Miss Mug
and her head starts to bleed.

It's the water race next.
Buckets filled to the brim.
You race down the track
and get soaked to the skin.

Sprots Day continues,
the egg-and-spoon's due.
Morag is cunning;
sticks her egg on . . . with glue.

Last relays are run
right round the school field.
Results are announced.
'Reds' win Cup *and* Shield!

We give a great shout,
hold Old Sam up high.
But wait, just look there.
Black clouds in the sky.

It's suddenly cold.
It suddenly pours.
And we're in our T-shirts
stuck out-of-doors.

It's three cheers for all,
for teachers as well,
then back into school,
running like hell!

First-aid tent's collapsed,
the chairs are all soaked.
There's litter, there's mud,
and the caretaker's choked.

Sprots Day is over.
A great afternoon!
There's thunder and lightning.
It's summer! It's June!

Trouble?

Has someone told? And if so, who?
   I sit on the hard bench outside
the Head's room, and I'm in a stew.
      See me now, the message said.
      Time's dragging. I wish I was dead.
Has someone told? And if so, who?

Am I in trouble, or what, *what*?
   The long corridor lies empty,
then a door slams like a pistol shot.
      Someone shouts. Faint cheers from the Hall.
      I stare at the pictures on the wall.
Am I in trouble, or what, *what*?

Who's been telling tales, and why, *why*?
   Muffled voices from the Head's room.
Mother told me: tell the truth, never lie.
      In her office the Secretary starts to sing.
      I hear the telephone ring and ring.
Who's been telling tales, and why, *why*?

What will happen? *Has* someone told?
   I fidget. Soon there is the chink
of cups and saucers. I feel cold.
      Up the corridor comes Andrea Line,
      sees me and gives the thumbs-down sign.
What will happen? *Has* someone told?

What's it about? Won't someone say?
   I've been here . . . hours. It's almost break.
My friends will soon go out to play.
      I've been forgotten. I feel ill.
      I'm in a state and I can't sit still.
What's it about? Oh, won't someone say?

Tracey's tree

Last year it was not there,
the sapling with purplish leaves
planted in our school grounds with care.
It's Tracey's tree, my friend who died,
and last year it was not there.

Tracey, the girl with long black hair
who, out playing one day, ran
across a main road for a dare.
The lorry struck her. Now a tree grows
and last year it was not there.

Through the classroom window I stare
and watch the sapling sway.
Soon its branches will stand bare.
It wears a forlorn and lonely look
and last year it was not there.

October's chill is in the air
and cold rain distorts my view.
I feel a sadness that's hard to bear.
The tree blurs, as if I've been crying,
and last year it was not there.

The Harvest Festival rehearsal

Miss Monkhouse, our teacher,
has blonde hair – metres of the stuff –
and wears clothes that look
as if they've been cut from a tent.
Today she's brought us to the Hall
to rehearse a poem,
our class's contribution
to the school's Harvest Festival event.

The caretaker's there,
puffing hard as he sets up the stage.
It's the usual collection
of wobbly, wonky, wooden blocks.
We climb up, laughing,
but Samantha trips,
bangs her nose against Jacko's knee.
Blood drips, drips onto her white socks.

At last we settle down,
tallest at the back,
those in front kneeling
until Allan Jones sneezes wetly . . . twice.
We all lean back, shout, 'Yerruck!'
Miss Monkhouse stamps her foot,
yells for quiet!
In her voice more than a hint of ice.

Now she rises on tip-toe,
arms raised as if she's
conducting a cathedral choir.
One, two, three, four . . . and we're off.
But no. Before a single word's spoken
Omar starts to splutter
like a fish with the 'flu. Miss fumes.
'Boy, go and get a drink for that cough!'

Omar runs out, choking.
We wait. Amanda burps.
The Headteacher walks in,
shakes her head and then walks out.
With luck we'll start soon.
Miss, again on tip-toe, says,
'Speak up. Speak clearly.
But never mumble or mutter or SHOUT!'

> *'Harvest time,*
> *Harvest time,*
> *It's harvest time*
> *Again.*
> *Seeds were sown,*
> *Crops have grown*
> *In the sun*
> *And rain.'*

'That was good,' says Miss,
'apart from you, Peter.
You were three words behind everyone.
Wake up, boy, you . . . you neddy!'
Now Jamila steps forward,
her pony tail swaying.
She has two verses to recite.
Miss Monkhouse asks her, 'Are you ready?'

> *'Fields so full*
> *Of golden wheat*
> *For the bread*
> *We love to eat.*
>
> *'Apples red,*
> *So smooth and round.*
> *THUMP THUMP THUMP*
> *They hit the ground.'*

Jamila steps back, all smiles.
Lisa pokes out her tongue,
Brian pinches her arm,
Someone gives her pony tail a tweak.
    'Miss, Miss!' Jamila bawls,
    'They're pulling my hair!'
    Miss Monkhouse clenches her teeth
and thinks . . . this is going to take *all week*!

Then, when we're set to proceed,
    Marion complains that she feels faint.
    'Miss,' she says feebly, 'I need fresh air.'
Our teacher's face sets in one big frown.
    But all's not lost.
    Here comes Leela and her curls.
    With her el-o-cu-tion voice
she'll not let Miss Monkhouse down.

> *'Tomatoes glow*
> *Like mini suns.*
> *Potatoes . . . tons*
> *And tons and tons.*
>
> *'In the sea*
> *A trillion fish.*
> *Haddock, kippers*
> *On my dish.'*

    'KIPPERS?' screeches Carl.
    The thought of them
    is enough to make him vomit.
'Miss, Carl's been . . . SICK!'
    The caretaker returns,
    cleans up the mess, looks grim.
    It seems hours, *hours* later
when Miss says, 'It's you now, Dick.'

> *'Bananas*
> *Yellow as the moon.*
> *Ummm,*
> *With cream upon my spoon.'*

('Ummmmmmm,' we have to say.
But some take a second,
Others half the day!)

'Soon it's conkers.
You play me.
Autumn leaves
Fall from the tree.'

(Falling leaves . . . we flap one hand.
Joshi gets slapped.
Miss doesn't seem to understand . . .)

Now it's Sandeep and Jeff.
They play a game of conkers
but neither can land a hit.
Miss groans, 'Really it should be a piece of cake!'
Outside it starts to pour
and playtime's due.
The rehearsal goes on, on.
The school field begins to look like a lake.

'Now the days
Grow short and blear.
Harvest's over.
Winter's here.'

Another delay. Shaun falls
off the wooden blocks
with a sound like a house collapsing
or a rumble of thunder.
Miss Monkhouse covers her eyes,
shakes her head
and wonders if this whole thing
is one huge monumental blunder.

But, it's too late
for thoughts like that.
Here comes finale time:
our Harvest Festival poem is nearly through.
Once more the stage is checked,
and Miss gives her final orders,
'Stand straight, no slouching,
try your *very* best . . . oh, *do*!'

> *'Gone the leaves,*
> *The sun's warm glow.*
> *Soon the wind,*
> *The ice, the snow.*
>
> *'Soon the wind*
> *The ice*
>
> *'The snow.'*

With our hands we mime
snowflakes falling.
There is silence.
Down, down, down drifts the snow.
It's effective,
we can all see that.
Miss Monkhouse smiles and says,
'Class, I think at last we have . . . a show!'

We stand, frozen,
no one moves, or even breathes.
Then we take a bow
and the Harvest poem is complete.
The bell rings.
Playtime!
And it's stopped raining!
Outside we race. Playtime! *Neat*!

Grey squirrel

Noses against the classroom windows,
teacher standing behind us, we stare out
as a grey squirrel nimbles its way
over the field's million sodden leaves
on this damp November day.

The trees drip, the grass is dank,
the playground shines like plastic.
A bedraggled sun. All's still, still,
except for that squirrel now busy
at husks of beech nuts, nibbling his fill.

Suddenly he's bolt upright, sniffing,
and then gone, swarming up a tree trunk
like Spiderman scaling a vertical wall.
Now he tight-rope-runs along a branch
and leaps to the next tree, does not fall.

We return to our tables. Chairs scrape.
Teacher stands at the board, chalk poised.
No one speaks. For a minute we secretly gloat
over the wonder of that squirrel
in leather gloves and grey fur coat.

Rhamphorhynchus

(the fish-eating, flying reptile)

Look,
        as he swoops from the cliff's rugged face
His squadrons of teeth instant death
To careless fish basking in shallow seas
        And lizards short of breath.

His tough skin is cracked and worn as old boots;
His cries blood-curdle the night.
A Dracula beast with claws on his wings
        He glides . . . the world's first kite.

The Pterosaurs' party

On a table of stone
there is blood, there is bone,
    a beast feast
when the Pterosaurs hold their
    wild party,
      their wild party.

They will play 'Peck your Neck'
then the furniture wreck,
    a wing ding
when the Pterosaurs hold their
    wild party,
      their wild party.

More guests come gliding in,
their shrill shrieks swell the din,
    a loud crowd
when the Pterosaurs hold their
    wild party,
      their wild party.

It goes on till the sun
shouts, 'A new day's begun!'
    A morn yawn
ends the Pterosaurs' wild, wild,
    wild party,
      their wild party.

Tyrannosaurus Rex

(the King of the tyrant lizards)

Two daft little arms like toasting forks,
    enough skin to make coats for ten men.
        As dirty as pitch
        (he slept rough in a ditch),
    and the feet from a monstrous hen.

A bit of a freak – part beast, part bird.
    Would you dare stick your tongue out at him?
        He's a mean dinosaur
        with a mouth wide as a door
    and teeth that stand up dagger-slim.

Across the mud flats he belts in top gear;
    a rogue lighthouse with blood on his brain.
        Better kneel down and pray
        for all those in his way:
    he'll grind bones again and again.

Plesiosaurus

(the swimming reptile)

He was the terror of the teeming seas,
had the head of a crocodile,
a speed-king from millions of years BC
with the first Jack-the-Ripper smile.

Air bubbles gasped at the swish of his tail,
his mouth was a drawer of sharp knives.
In waves tinged with blood his flippers flail-flailed,
and fish fled from his deep-sea dives.

It must have been tough, all that searching for grub,
no time just to float or to play.
When he died Plessy sank through the sea like a sub.
In deep mud his whitened bones lay.

A box of fireworks

Silver rain

    Our gentlest rain,
Soft as a house with foam walls,
It paints the damp grass silver
      Where its fire falls.

Giant rocket

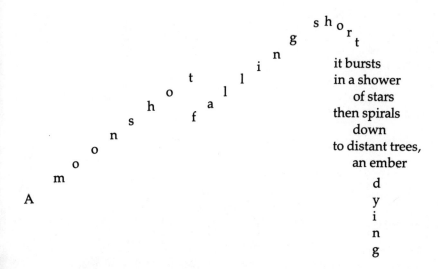

it bursts
in a shower
of stars
then spirals
down
to distant trees,
an ember
d
y
i
n
g

Catherine wheel

To the bonfire's
loud crackle
and the shrill squeals
of girls
the fiery fossil
whizzes and fizzles
and whirls.

Saint Catherine,
too,
must have shrieked
but with pain
as the Wheel of Fire
tore her
again and again.

Our firework dies,
is knocked
from its post
but its smoke
fills the night
with Catherine's
ghost.

Sparkler

A magic stick,
    Guy Fawkes' wand,
held tight
    in a thick-gloved hand.

Blooming at night,
    a rose from Mars:
the 'Fizzer',
    my 'Maker of Stars'.

56

Jumping Jack

This is the wild one
   (LOOK OUT!)
unpredictable
as Brian Clough
   (CAREFUL!)
and a real eater
of toes.

It goes mad
at a lick of flame
   (STAND BACK!)
and is a distant cousin
   (WATCH IT!)
of the Mercurian
glass-hopper.

Like a crackle
of rifle fire
   (IT'S COMING!)
it leaps, leaps
through the night
   (RUN! RUN!)
seeking you out.

Scatter!
Run!

It's got the scent
of your
Wellington Boots!

Carolling around the estate

The six of us met at Alan's house
   and Jane brought a carol sheet
that she'd got free from the butcher's shop
   when she bought the Sunday meat.

Sanjit had a new lantern light
   made by his Uncle Sed,
and Jim had 'borrowed' his dad's new torch
   which flashed white, green and red.

Our first call was at Stew Foster's place
   where we sang 'Three Kings' real well
but his mother couldn't stand the row
   and she really gave us hell!

We drifted on from door to door
   singing carols by lantern light.
Jane's lips were purple with the cold;
   my fingers were turning white.

Around nine we reached the 'Chippy' shop
   where we ordered pies and peas,
and with hot grease running down our hands
   we started to de-freeze.

I reached home tired out, but my mum said,
   'Your cousin Anne's been here.
She's carolling tomorrow night
   and I said you'd go, my dear.'

Still

Snow, finer than crushed glass
falls continuously
smothering road and roof
until the day shivers
to a Christmas card still.

Buried, the earth's slowed pulse
weathers this deep season.

Visitor

Sliding in slippers along the house-side
you find fragments of the turkey's carcass
beside the toppled dustbin lid, and there
on the lawn's snow quilt, a line of paw marks.

Town fox, that wraith of winter, soundlessly
thieved here as frost bit hard and stars shivered.
This bleak morning, under a raw-boned sky,
you stoop to examine the frozen tracks,

and print yours where a spectral guest came late
to share a Christmas dinner. Around the
gable-end a starved wind razors and from
the split gutters icicles hang like fangs.

A short cut . . . after dark

It's late.
The night is icy
as we head for home
after carol singing,
coins chinking in our collecting tin.
It's so cold.
Our fingers feel frost-bitten.
The estate is quiet,
there's no one about.
Snow lies on the pavement.
Far away a dog barks.

It's late.
We decide to take a short cut
through the school grounds.
So, climb the wall, drop,
and race past the 'No Trespassers' sign,
race past the skeleton trees,
the bushes hunched
like sleeping bears.
Beneath our boots
the crisp snow creaks.
So dark, so dark.

It's late.
Hearts thumping,
we stop, breathless,
at the school building.
We inhale fast
and the freezing air
hurts our lungs.
Listen! An owl hoots.
In the clear sky a million stars
are like silver nails hammered into the hull
of a vast, black ship.

It's late.
The last lap. Wraith-like we skate
across the playground
and vault the padlocked gate.
At last, we reach our street.
No cars. No people.
Three days before Christmas
and our carols long gone
into the frozen night.
Home. Lights in the hall. Warmth.
It's late.

The snowman

Child's play:
  stacked snow,
   scarf, hat,
    carrot nose,
     stick and
      round pebbles
      for eyes.

    He freezes:
   fat target
   for snowballers
  who dearly
  want to
 knock off
his block.

Three days,
 and grey
  with age
   he shrinks
    as warmth
    turns the
     world green.

    Scarf, hat
   are reclaimed.
  Pebbles mark
 his grave,
damp lawn
where a
child plays.